Creatures of the Forest Habitat

Porcupines

Sebastian Avery

PowerKiDS press.

New York

Published in 2017 by The Rosen Publishing Group, Inc.
29 East 21st Street, New York, NY 10010

First Edition

Editor: Caitie McAneney
Book Design: Mickey Harmon

Photo Credits: Cover (series logo) iLoveCoffeeDesign/Shutterstock.com; cover, pp. 1, 3, 4, 6, 8, 10, 12, 14, 16, 18, 20, 22—24 (background) BlueRingMedia/Shutterstock.com; cover (porcupine) Blake Kent/Design Pics/Getty Images; p. 5 BGSmith/Shutterstock.com; p. 6 https://commons.wikimedia.org/wiki/File:Mexican-hairy-porcupine-1.jpg; p. 7 angelshot/Shutterstock.com; p. 9 Maria Jeffs/Shutterstock.com; p. 10 jeep2499/Shutterstock.com; p. 11 (inset) Lisa Hagan/Shutterstock.com; p. 11 (main) Robert Haasmann/Shutterstock.com; p. 13 Scenic Shutterbug/Shutterstock.com; p. 15 Geoffrey Kuchera/Shutterstock.com; p. 17 (main),22 critterbiz/Shutterstock.com; p. 17 (wolverine) Erik Mandre/Shutterstock.com; p. 17 (owl) Theresa Lauria/Shutterstock.com; p. 19 CREATISTA/Shutterstock.com; p. 21 Radius Images/Getty Images.

Cataloging-in-Publication Data

Names: Avery, Sebastian.
Title: Porcupines / Sebastian Avery.
Description: New York : PowerKids Press, 2017. | Series: Creatures of the forest habitat | Includes index.
Identifiers: ISBN 9781499427578 (pbk.) | ISBN 9781499429275 (library bound) | ISBN 9781499427158 (6 pack)
Subjects: LCSH: Porcupines–Juvenile literature.
Classification: LCC QL737.R652 A94 2017 | DDC 599.35'97–dc23

Manufactured in the United States of America

CPSIA Compliance Information: Batch #BW17PK: For Further Information contact Rosen Publishing, New York, New York at 1-800-237-9932

Contents

The Prickly Porcupine

The porcupine is the sharpest animal in the forest! These forest **rodents** are covered in sharp quills. The quills are like needles, and they are the porcupine's best **defense** against predators.

There are more than 20 species, or kinds, of porcupines in the world. The one you might be familiar with is the North American porcupine, or common porcupine. This is the only species of porcupine that you'll find in the United States. This book focuses on the North American porcupine.

Forest Friend Facts

The name "porcupine" comes from the Latin words that roughly mean "quill pig" or "thorn pig."

This porcupine loves to hang out in trees!

5

Porcupines on the Map

There are two major kinds of porcupines—Old World and New World. Old World porcupines live in Africa, Southeast Asia, and southern Europe. Long-tailed porcupines and African crested porcupines are types of Old World porcupines. New World porcupines live in South America, Central America, and North America. They include Mexican hairy dwarf porcupines and North American porcupines.

North American porcupines have a very wide **range**. They're found in the northeastern and western United States. They live as far north as the Great Lakes, Canada, and Alaska.

Forest Friend Facts

The Mexican hairy dwarf porcupine is found in central Mexico and as far south as Panama.

North American porcupines are also called Canadian porcupines.

Porcupine Habitats

Forests are perfect **habitats** for porcupines. Many porcupines live almost entirely in trees. They use trees for both food and shelter, and they're great at climbing. Other porcupines spend more time on the ground, especially if there are grasses and plants to hide under.

Some porcupines live where there are few trees at all. Porcupines can be found in deserts and even the **tundra**. They are very adaptable, which means they can change to fit their surroundings. They can survive in both warm and cold **regions**.

Forest Friend Facts

Porcupines that live in the Rocky Mountains often spend their time in ponderosa pine trees.

Porcupines often fall out of trees because they love to eat the tender buds and twigs at the end of branches.

Tree Dwellers

North American porcupines are one of the largest porcupine species in the world. They can grow up to 3 feet (0.9 m) long with a 10-inch (25.4 cm) tail. They can weigh up to 35 pounds (15.9 kg). Each porcupine may have more than 30,000 quills covering its body.

Porcupines are built to live in trees. They have long front teeth, like most rodents. They use these teeth to **gnaw** on wood. Porcupines have **stout** bodies and they walk slowly on land, but they're great at climbing.

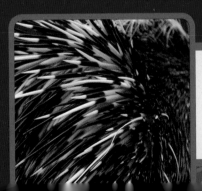

Forest Friend Facts

Porcupines have short brown or black fur between their quills.

opossum

Like another forest dweller, the opossum, some porcupines have tails that can grip tree limbs while they're climbing.

The Life of a Porcupine

Porcupines like to live alone. That makes them solitary animals. However, males and females come together to **mate** each year.

Mother porcupines usually only give birth to one baby at a time. They take care of their baby until it's around two months old. They feed the baby milk and keep it safe. Eventually, the baby will leave its mother. At around two years old porcupines are ready to start having babies of their own. A group of porcupines is called a family.

Forest Friend Facts

Baby porcupines are called porcupettes.

Baby porcupines have quills, too. They're soft at first, but they grow sharp and hard a few days after birth.

Ouch!

You don't want to be stuck with a porcupine quill. Porcupines raise their quills when they feel scared. If a predator touches or bites the porcupine, the sharp quills stab the predator. They detach, or separate, from the porcupine. The predator may end up with a face full of sharp, needlelike quills.

Porcupine quills have barbs on them. Barbs are hooks that make the quill hard to pull from an enemy's skin. It's very painful, which makes quills a great defense for porcupines.

Forest Friend Facts

What happens when a porcupine loses its quills in an attack? It grows new ones!

When a porcupine doesn't feel threatened, its quills are usually flat on its back.

15

Porcupine Predators

Just because porcupines have a great defense doesn't mean they don't have predators. One porcupine predator is the fisher. Fishers are small **mammals** in the weasel family. They know how to flip a porcupine on its back and attack its quill-less belly. In some places, porcupine populations are rising to an unhealthy amount. Scientists bring fishers into these areas to decrease the porcupine population.

Porcupines are also targeted by birds of prey such as eagles and great horned owls. Mammals such as martens and wolverines might also attack them.

Porcupine predators need to have a special plan in place. One wrong move can mean being stuck with dozens of quills.

wolverine

great horned owl

fisher

17

Wood Eaters

Porcupines have big teeth for a reason. They help the porcupine chew on all sorts of wood. You may find a porcupine gnawing on tree bark. You can tell which trees porcupines have eaten from because the bark is stripped from the trunk. This sometimes kills trees, so some people think porcupines are **pests**.

Porcupines also eat other plant parts, such as flower buds, fruit, stems, and seeds. They use their sharp teeth to crack nuts.

Forest Friend Facts

Most porcupines are herbivores, or animals that eat only plants. However, some porcupines eat small lizards and bugs.

Forests have all the food
a porcupine needs!

19

Porcupines and People

It's likely that you'll never come in contact with a porcupine. That's because they usually only come out at night. That makes them nocturnal. During the day, when people are awake, the porcupine would rather stay in its underground **burrow** or hide up in a tree.

If you do see a porcupine, don't touch it! Porcupines won't attack you, but if you touch one, you will get stuck with its quills. This is usually less of a problem for people than it is for curious pet dogs.

Forest Friend Facts

Porcupines can't shoot their quills at you. That's just a **myth**!

If you think there's a porcupine living near you, keep your pets inside at night. You don't want them to end up covered in quills!

Porcupines Need the Forest

Porcupine populations are not in danger at this time. However, their habitats are at risk. Forest habitats are under constant danger from the logging industry. Some forests are cleared to make room for new neighborhoods or for large farms. Taking away the trees means taking away porcupines' homes.

Porcupines are made to live in the forest. They are some of the greatest tree lovers around. It's important to keep the forests safe so porcupines and other forest creatures can continue to live in peace.

Glossary

burrow: A hole an animal digs in the ground for shelter.

defense: A feature of a living thing that helps keep it safe.

gnaw: To bite or chew repeatedly.

habitat: The natural place where an animal or plant lives.

mammal: A warm-blooded animal that has a backbone and hair, breathes air, and feeds milk to its young.

mate: To come together to make babies.

myth: An idea or story that's believed by many people but isn't true.

pest: A creature that causes problems for people.

range: The area where something lives.

region: A large area of land that has a number of features in common.

rodent: A small, furry animal with large front teeth, such as a mouse or rat.

stout: Having a short and strong body.

tundra: Cold northern lands that lack forests and have permanently

Index

Websites

Due to the changing nature of Internet links, PowerKids Press has developed an online list of websites related to the subject of this book. This site is updated regularly. Please use this link to access the list: www.powerkidslinks.com/forest/porc